D. E. Lawrence has been a business coach, sports professional, educator, and diversity and inclusion advisor/trainer for several years and has an international practice covering the USA, UK, EU and the Caribbean. His current interests include groupwork, sports management , jazz composition and being an ally to sports and arts projects that support young people and the reduction of knife and gun crime.

This book is dedicated to my lovely daughters, my ever curious and beautiful granddaughters and Althea Davis, my inspirational childhood school principal and a very dear friend, may she and Angel rest in peace. Thanks for helping me to see the benefits of being helpful to others, even when there is a storm on the horizon and there is always a *storm*.

D. E. Lawrence

OWNING, GROWING AND BEING

AUSTIN MACAULEY PUBLISHERS™

LONDON • CAMBRIDGE • NEW YORK • SHARJAH

A CIP catalogue record for this title is available from the British Library.

ISBN 9781398493780 (Paperback)
ISBN 9781398493797 (ePub e-book)

www.austinmacauley.com

First Published 2024
Austin Macauley Publishers Ltd®
1 Canada Square
Canary Wharf
London
E14 5AA

This book would never have 'gotten off the planner' if it was not for the book's volunteer focus group... even the pandemic did not stop us... you all rock!

Table of Contents

Foreword

A lived Experience

What is my story…is it something that has a beginning, a middle or an end? I had no choice whatsoever to have been born, that decision was with the universe and whoever she must answer to.

Many different people around me, some old and some not so old…we have treated each other the way that we have, it is now set within our chapters of our life stories and our new and old life moment.

In the end we have only added to each other's lived experiences with no way to erase the bad moments in order to only highlight just the good, the great and the happy moments…all still there.

As I learn and grew, I see more into my heart and into my soul…it's actually quite amazing how my vulnerable things are looking in there from this vantage point. My memories of hope and my recollections of the joy, these times, they are allowed to shine through, the only things that are really mine… my lived experiences are like a beacon that shows the route through my loving memories, accessing the names and the memories that will soon grow into the haze of old age.

The thorny expressions of unwanted hate, unfair actions, and thoughts, they are all there too...these have grown quickly in certain areas, like an very unwanted cancer, they stain, move on stain again and never seem to morph into a hazy memory ...yes, these are my lived experience too.

As the days and nights begin to grow shorter, my stories seem to look for the exit signs, to find their final large, big fluffy duvet to head under for warmth, comfort and a place of rest.

The regret basket has gotten less things in it now as the days and months have now moved on to years now. Myself I just want those that have shown love to me and mine to keep our memories for as long as you can...continue as hard as you can to keep them. For those that I have loved and owe mountains of gratitude, I have tried to do the same.

For those that have tried to add the pain, force rewrites onto a life that was never yours, I wish that hope and joy overwhelm you and yours enough to permanently distract you from whatever has drawn you to me, mine and others.

A lived Experience by 'Robert'

What Difference Does My Past, Present and Future Experiences Make: Why This Book?

What is 'a lived experience', and does it really matter to you in your everyday life and perhaps maybe how you see yourself today?

When you wake up each morning, what things concern you...about yourself...what things concern you about others around you? Does what you think about, and what you experience each day really matter...who says? Does what others think that you think about, and what they think that you experience really matter...who says?

In places where we might give and or receive support and assistance to/from others, say such as at an advice centre, at a sexual health clinic, at a mother and baby unit, at a foster home, at a youth club, at a food bank, at a hospital, with a 'clued up' best friend, at a church, at a mosque, a synagogue, a school, a health clinic, etc. *staff, volunteers and their service users might talk about these type of questions* that are mentioned above at least *several times a* week and potentially so might think about them *almost daily...what do you think?*

Are you 'a helper' or 'a person that provided and or receives regular support from others'?

For a lot of us, the 'global beings', most of us are genuinely nice, civil, thoughtful, considerate and will provide assistance to others where and when we can. *Is our care and consideration 'unconditional' or is it and or can it be based up how were feelings about 'the composition of others' lives 'in those moments'.* Maybe at times we might often use 'our assumptions' about various 'peoples stories', e.g. "...he probably is new to the country...maybe they have more children than they can handle...I wonder if they were in the care system as children...they were probably bullied as a child...they look like they could use 'a break'...being that colour, they must get harassed every day...they probably already get enough government benefits, they should not be here...".

The potential 'stories' and 'personal experiences' of those that receives and or provide services could be endless...*do you have a story?*

For those that may have read some of the things that we have written about over the years[1], they will then know that we try to use research and or action research basis for most of our academic publications. Having sources to draw upon from real life experiences across the global range of diversity, this really does matter to us, hopefully our readers will continue to appreciate this fact as well.

---

[1] Criminal justice, education, group work, addiction, managing aggressive situations, leadership, team work, young people, men, equality, diversity and inclusion, etc.

We also try to be of use to those that are trying to develop new skills and insights within their professions, and or their paid and unpaid workplaces and or perhaps even for their own personal self-awareness gains. Everyone is different and has their own reasons for entering into a personal and professional programme of study.

For our more 'CPD[2] related' publications[3] such as this one, we also use 'informal focus groups'[4] and or have added 'practical composite mini case study characters' within our articles and publications with sole intentions to summarise some of the views of hundreds of people that we have gathered from all over the world without ever using any real names.

This book, while much smaller in word count than some of our previous publications, it still is based upon the views of 'real people'[5] and draws upon some of our own personal and professional experiences as well. The topic *'A Lived Experience'* seems to be a growing one, for us this book had its early roots as a 2021 podcast CPD training script in the UK before then being developed into a paper and then by popular demand was then developed into the small book that you are reading today, one with self-paced reading material that is then followed up with 'thought questions' which are added throughout each chapter for your consideration. 'COELD

---

[2] Continuing Professional Development, etc.

[3] Chapters, articles, papers, unpublished papers, etc.

[4] Made up of friends, associates, professional colleagues, etc. (but always arising from their diverse life experiences and their generous spirits).

[5] Via informal focus groups October-November 2021.

philosophy'[6]; **C**reating **O**pportunities for **E**xploring, **L**earning and **D**evelopment are very important to us.

Several of the focus group members strongly pointed out that while they might not have always agreed about the roots of racism and or discrimination within the UK (for example), they unanimously agreed that 'different people can and do have/had different experiences' to each other and that often this 'individual experience' can be demonstrated, illustrated and or otherwise expressed through a person's level of efforts, energy (or lack of), emotions, their expressions of being joyous and or the complete opposite e.g. being unhappy, angry, unheard and maybe often even feeling and or actually being unrecognised within their own communities, not feeling as being something of worth, and as such, perhaps these same individuals should be invested in and further developed[7] and maybe be even given 'chances' and 'additional opportunities' after getting to know more about their own lives and its[8] impact on their ability to live their best lives ,while also becoming more positive and active citizens.

The notion that the *act of listening to and the act of considering* of the impact that one's life has a much *more (potentially) helpful and self-sustaining* basis than simply saying that they (individuals, their families, their communities, etc.) are 'a product of' say, 'racism', 'internalised racism', 'sexism', 'ageism', 'classism'…and these same latter terms and phrases when used can often then

---

[6] COELD, used by permission of Diversity Management LCL

[7] To become more employable, etc.

[8] Their 'lives', etc.

used to 'label us' and ' put us into boxes' that can then easily be 'explained away' by 'bullet points' on a flip chart perhaps[9].

This book is part of an on-going and a very much evolving series of books that look at diverse relationships within the context of everyday living.

It has two parts. **This book** *that you are reading at the moment, and it is followed directly by a short* **training programme***, one that could be useful to you. You could enjoy it over a nice cup of tea (or whatever your favourite hot drink is), or maybe complete it with your work team, whatever you do is fine. Often people complete the training and then pass on their learning to their work colleagues that have not completed the training.*

The hope is that by honestly looking at some of the issues and concerns that have and may continue to challenge 'real' individuals, partners, families, communities and professionals within their general everyday relationships[10] , that these same explored relationships can improve and go on to greatly enhance the quality[11] of our own lives, as 'global beings', especially where in the past some of us might have felt 'unheard' and 'or maybe even not included' at times , and this

---

[9] Often within social work courses, counselling courses, legal courses, medical courses, etc.

[10] This includes educators, social workers, social care, youth workers, sports coaches, coaches, parents, carers, couples, friends, etc.

[11] Self-defined, with regard to what 'a life', etc. might look and feel like.

would be regardless of our race, our cultures, our genders, our sexual orientation, our class, our learning styles and abilities, our size and or shapes, our physical and medical status, etc..

Some Personal Reflections

I have had diverse paid and unpaid work experiences within the US, UK, EU and in the Caribbean. I remember going into 'professional meetings[12] 'recently , either as 'an ally' for someone or for a job-related meeting or similar. In these meetings at least one of the 'professionals' in the room usually looks at me and acknowledges me via 'a non-verbal language nod', one where I usually 'easily understood' (or assumed that I had actually understood) what they meant, each and every time that they did 'the nod'[13].

However, when they generally used the verbal phrase 'a lived experience' within the same conversations about someone that I might have been an ally to and or when these same professional people were discussing something about me, it was then that 'something different' seemed to be happening, where my feelings of 'confusion and or my feelings of being unsettled' began to occur 'big time' and this was usually felt 'from my head as a mild headache, running down to a what felt like 'a sucker punch' to my stomach, and ending right down at my very large feet'!

Initially I think that I got very uncomfortable feelings inside because I did not know what the #%!!! that they, the

---

[12] Such as related to counselling, business mentoring and or coaching, educational support sessions, family support, etc.

[13] Over my lifetime, in most cases since childhood, the 'nod' was usually from 'another person of colour'

'professionals in the room' were specifically talking about or what their 'intentions' were during those particular moments.

They knew very little about the people that I was associated with on those particular occasions, and they knew even less about me as a particular person and or as a professional, so what are they going on about 'in this moment'? Were they trying to make us (or just me) feel more at ease, to maybe 'add more value' to themselves, those 'professionals' in the meeting, and or maybe to just simply trying to make us all feel less threatened and potentially 'more heard and more understood early on' within those 'meeting moments'?

Even more suspiciously, I was thinking to myself, like 'a revolving door of thoughts' actually e.g. "…why didn't they use the phrase 'a lived experience' when they introduced themselves and or when they introduced their role(s) to us???…".

If there is 'an assumed connection' here, then surely this could have been highlighted much earlier on within 'a positive communication space'.

I wonder what do our readers think…should 'the professionals' come clean about their assumptions, and intention early on within any 'discussion space'? Would doing so or not doing so, help and or hinder 'the communication' and or the 'mutual assumption space'? Y/N Explain:

My curiosity continued to peak over the next few months about what I thought was the 'basis and the intent' of this 'peculiar phrase'… 'a lived experience'. From my experience it was usually used in conversations and 'marketing blogs' by white professionals and helpers about their potential (the organisation) and or sometimes when describing their actual non-white service users, non-white beneficiaries, and or non-white clients.

In years past I would have described this using my personal and professional 'filters' as 'making limited assumptions' by the professionals and then they (professionals with good intentions) maybe continue attaching 'crazy attributions' based upon limited information such as 'wishful thinking', skin colour, language, body shape/size, hairstyles, immigration status, the way people might have been dressed, maybe the use of the 'phrase ex-offender', employment status, etc. but somehow, I think these professionals might have 'meant something more' than this.

I am not generally considered a 'paranoid' person, but more of a 'curious one', something that I have learned to become proud of and see it as one of 'my added values' as a global being.

There are other relatively new terms and phrases such as 'intersectionality', e.g. considering where race, class, gender, and other individual characteristics 'intersect' with one another and overlap…genuinely another very useful and interesting way of looking at global diversity and the 'interconnectedness' of the challenges for global beings in their daily lives.

Being a gospel, soul, and blues musician since my childhood, I was always around very large and small groups of people and loved listening to their 'nonverbal' conversations to me and around me. This 'watching and listening' (verbally and non-verbally) to other individuals, and other groups of people, especially when they think that no one else is watching or listening developed into my professional observation and assessment skills. During some of those 'observed moments', these same viewed people in recent months only used the phrase 'a lived experience' when they were talking about themselves (sometimes connected to race, culture, religion, sexuality, lifestyles, etc). During these same moments those around them in the same communication space that were listening very respectfully, intently and rarely challenging their use of such a phrase, it was like everyone in 'the discussion space', that they all seemed to have 'instinctively known' what this phrase meant and or they all understood what this expression meant and that this phrase was somehow 'virtually untouchable' and all of those present seem to instinctively knew this, 'almost without words' and had non verbally expressed this often within this space, and that it would and could be somehow be viewed as being disrespectful to somehow interject someone else's views, thoughts or insights into the discussion, to those moments…very curious indeed!

I have been on several job interviews and or professional conferences related to counselling psychology and there was always at least one professional that only wanted their '(lived) experiences to matter', to only hear the sound of their own voice(s) and 'made it very, very clear to not butt in' and or for us as listeners and observers to not have a more exciting life story to add and or have more in-depth comments (than theirs) to contribute because it was not at all encouraged and it was definitely not going to be valued, regardless of any sound and interesting validity that could have come out from extra voices and or from having any other 'lived experience backed up stories' that others might come with.

> *Have any of our readers met individuals such as this[14]...how might you feel being in 'their presence' during these moments? Did 'the relationship quality develop' into a more 'mutually rewarding one', or did it stay the same (or become worse), say as within your 'initial encounter' with people in situations such as described above?*

I have several poets and slam artist friends that reside all over the world, they were generally quite helpful in developing my understanding here. They come from all over the world, from small and large cities, but they all seem to have some sort of 'universal and or linked spiritual connection' that connects them together.

Most of them said that 'a lived experience' meant that you had developed 'your own road map' just from waking up each day and living out the minutes of your existence, even if you stayed in bed all day, your thinking, and your own experiencing...and any 'recollections and after thoughts' were exclusively just yours too and no one else's ...just your lived experiences.

They regularly wrote, performed and spoke about these lived experiences often with so much passion and expression, although sometimes the range of expression would flow and change like a meandering river...sometimes as an audience member you'd want to shout out with joy, sometimes maybe

---

[14] Those illustrated above, etc.

turn inwards with sorrow, anger, maybe even despair, feelings and images, all based around their recollections of their own individual lived experiences and how they were 'interpreting it in those very moments'…a lived experience.

For a lot of us we wake up each day living, thinking, and experiencing things related to 'us', such as race, to sexuality, to gender, to class, to language, to our learning difficulties, learning styles, to our physical and medical conditions, to our various 1-1 and group relating to others, to our experiences within those that we might call our family, our friends, within our interactions to and reactions with various parts of the general area, and or local communities , and or national scene , and maybe within the wider international society, etc.

So as my poet friends and colleagues might say, 'these all belong to me'…and they also clearly say that these also 'belonged to "us"…'and 'the others', the billions of lived experiences of all of us co-existing on this little planet called Earth. We will explore this more in depth in future chapters.

Some interesting terms and phrases to consider and discuss:

Ally/Resource/Helper. A person who might be able to positively support us, assist us and increase our chances of positive success.

Creating Opportunities for Exploring Learning and Development (COELD)[15]. A method/framework for working within a multi-disciplinary care sector. Its primary aim is to put 'positive relationship insights' first … with each other,

---

15 Used by permission of Diversity Management LCL/Consider Celebrating Diversity and Sport 2021

with our service users, and with other professionals, when considering the skills, knowledge and awareness that are most desirable, personally and professionally, within the 'wider vocation' of social care, which encompasses volunteer work, counselling, mental health, education, criminal justice, youth work, social work, social care and psychology.

Ideally, a trainee practitioner/helper will learn that person centeredness and psychodynamic/psychological traditions are not always 'black and white', that at times they have 'shades of grey' and can be influenced by a variety of factors; the level of practitioner competence, the level of practitioner personal and/or professional insight, values and preferences, the needs and preferences of users and agencies, practice advances within the sector, and changing needs of the sector.

Diversity. Psychological, physical, social, learning, and theoretical differences and similarities that occur among individuals. These include areas such as race, colour, ethnicity, age, nationality, religion, socioeconomic status, parenting status, education, marital status, language, food choices, dress, gender, gender expression, gender identity, sexual orientation, learning styles, mental and physical abilities, genetic information, and learning styles.

Ideally personal and professional developments can be enhanced by participating in diverse aware training and education programmes, social care training, and counselling development frameworks that are aware 'by design' of the individual client's cultural values, beliefs and practices, and are sensitive to the environment from which the individual comes from and to the potential environment in which the individual may ultimately return.

Ego. In this instance, we are referring to a person's sense of importance and self-worth.

Often practitioners/helpers see themselves and their potential services users as having either a 'positive sense of ego' – where we see ourselves as not having any reason to look down on others in order to make us feel a more unrealistic and inflated sense of worth – or as having an 'unhealthy ego', where we see those around us potentially being not as good, intelligent, or as worthy as us in certain instances.

Respect. The feeling or understanding that someone or something is important, valued, and should be treated in a dignified way.

World centrism. The idea that one is concerned with the welfare of all global beings, and appreciates the range and richness of global difference and diversity that exists around the planet.

Chapter Conclusion

This expression, 'a lived experience' is quite an interesting one, to some quite a powerful phrase, one that this book tries to respectfully explore and consider within a non-academic and a non-jargonistic manner...this and the other books within the series aren't meant to just be used within colleges and universities for example, but hopefully also used at your workplaces or shared around the family dinner table, maybe discussed between friends at the local coffee shop, maybe added to continuing personal and professional development conferences, used within coaching and mentoring training, teacher training and especially explored within religious, cultural groups, youth work settings.

We also suggest that only those over the age of 16 should read this book and or be accepted upon any related CPD and training group. Some of the issues explored within the book might cause distress.

In latest versions we have added a brief CPD podcast Example/Training programme outline, one that could be useful to those that train and or support (including CPD providers) mentors, volunteers, youth workers, social workers, probation staff, education staff, coaches, politicians and any other paid and unpaid 'people to people' roles.

In the next chapter, we will explore some of the 'assumptions' within this book and its follow on training programme related to the phrase ' a lived experience'.

We all, as global beings matter very much!

Assumptions for This Book

In this book, the term 'a lived experience' and this book's premise is based upon several inter-related assumptions that we have made such as;

Assumptions

Assumption: These experience(s) are the types that will definitely bring up a range of global being thoughts, and a range of expressed individual and or group global being emotions and feelings too, maybe even some moments that could even lead to the 'unleashing of non-focused emotions' and or maybe 'a series of self-talk' , maybe sometimes this might be shown through personal and individual moments that could be considered by some as being very traumatic, provoking anger, sadness, unhappiness and maybe even bring out confusing and conflicting personal views and or recollections, etc.. Either way, the roots of these 'lived experiences' may not all be our fault, some will definitely be of our own making, but they all most certainly belong to us all now and forever more and it could be useful to come to terms with this fact.

They ('lived experiences') potentially also provide an opportunity and or 'a personal gateway' for further personal growth and development. With each of life's opportunities, whether or not that we choose to take them, this is totally up to us.

Assumption: Our lived experiences make us who we are, but thankfully they do not have to permanently define us…often an understanding of this one fact alone takes a long while for us as global beings to own up to. Sometimes we might wish to even hide our experiences away somewhere deep within our hearts and souls, often we rewrite these experiences and their impact upon us in our heads and or maybe even then creating a 'villain' of our stories. During these moments our lived experiences may becoming detached from us and or appear detached from us, it could be 'like these lives might belong to others' and maybe not really belong to us and at times could feel like they had never even existed.

Assumption: Life can be hard at times… we all respond and adjust to it in our own ways.

Assumption: Thankfully, there is more than just one way to 'grow and respond' as a global being…we can potentially have a 'life reset' as often as we may want to and or may need to, depending on the level of our own self-awareness and or the depth of our own intentions and or the depth of the life challenge and or the size of the life opportunity that is in front of us.

Assumption: Sometimes our reactions may seem like 'involuntary actions/reactions and thoughts', like we have no control over them at times or that at times maybe we even can't take no responsibility whatsoever for them either (our reactions). Some European centric approaches like psychotherapy link this to our experience of our 'parents/carers', to our 'our childhood experiences' and to 'our learning process and the levels of our development'.

Some 'wide ranging diverse thinkers and philosophers' link these experiences to what is going on within 'the society' that we live in (locally, regionally, nationally and globally), to our levels of 'personal active citizenship' and to the 'dynamic' of the ever-changing world around us'[16].

Usually, whatever perspective that we may lean towards, they often say that we have some range of 'choice' and or some range of 'self-power' (via personal development activities, via family involvements, friendships, cultural participation, religious affirmations, self-care, local, regional and national political systems involvements, etc.) to then take some control over 'our past and our present thoughts, and emotions. Continuing on with this thinking, we then can have some influence on 'the future us', at least by how we respond to our current and future thoughts, our current and future experiences, and the future events that are unfolding around us.

Assumption: Life can be satisfying at times[17].

Assumption: Life can have moments of hope[18].

Assumption: Life can have moments of joy[19].

Assumption: Life can have opportunities to support others.

---

[16] Say with regard to wealth, poverty, wars, oppression, natural and 'global being made' disasters, etc.

[17] These are all self-defined

[18] These are all self-defined

[19] These are all self-defined

Assumption: Life can have opportunities to be supported by others.

Additionally, from the authors point of view **'A lived experience' refers to** 'an **accumulation of individual experiences from our daily life existence, regardless of our age and or our physical state and or our financial situations , experiences that may have brought on deep and intense range of conscious and or unconscious physical and or emotional "energy"** ' such as related to trauma, stress, psychological and or emotional fracturing, periods of elation, happiness, joy, anxiety, fear, confusion, physical distress, related to my self-image and self-esteem etc …I am sure that there are other types of energies that I missed…please let me know so we can update our future editions of this book.

Assumption: In an 'ideal world', the assumption is (that for ourselves individually) **'I' have learned to acknowledge** (verbally, non-verbally, in writings, art, songs, hobbies, lifestyles, dreams, nightmares, during 'my quiet and my loud times', etc.) **that certain experiences have actually happened** within my own life (some of these which could be viewed as 'positive' and or 'not so positively' experience[ed]) and **that I can choose to do nothing with** them, **choose to use them for my own personal development and growth** or that I can also **choose to use them in my daily life for a variety of other life activities,** these could include getting others to directly and or indirectly maybe 'feel sorry for me' and or 'to make them feel responsible for me and my feelings'.

Assumption: Often several global beings work through these experiences and or offer these same experiences up within their mentorships/internships, volunteering, wor specialisms (such as counselling, mentoring, coaching, teaching, social work, youth work, medical professions, sports and health coaching, ministering to others, etc.), participation in politics, writing of chapters, articles and books, etc..

Assumption: Often for some of us, **these experiences are 'activated' and or used within our daily lives** and **can (and might) at times block**, predict, and or limit 'my' potential chances of happiness and or limit my potential expressions of joy within my current life (**'the now'**).

Assumption: (closely related to the last assumption) **These 'issues' and or my way of thinking about them** (often related to the past/present social, physical, emotive life challenges and or other related health and life challenges for ourselves and or others around us such as family, friends, partners, etc.) **may get in the way of 'the now'** (where my perceptions of moments, hope, happiness, joy, peace, 'so soness', etc. reside within me) **and potentially also get in the way of how we might perceive 'others' sense of 'their now'**.

Assumption: Some see 'a lived experience' in the context of their families and the context of those around them physically and or maybe even spiritually, and for some within the context of their self-described cultures, religions and or traditions. There is no 'right' or 'wrong' here. Several 'indigenous groups' ('the original peoples') may often take this perspective, even when 'the establishment' around them might not share their philosophies, lifestyles, and expressions and or might not even value their lived experiences, ones that are 'backed up' within thousands of years' worth of 'lived and community histories', contributions, and levels of personal and community power.

Some Interesting Terms and Phrases to Consider and Discuss:

Ability. The power or capacity to do or act – individually and within a group(s) – spiritually, emotionally, physically, mentally, legally, morally, and financially.

Emotional competency. Being able to know one's emotions. For example, consider what it is like to be 'happy', 'mad', 'glad', 'sad', 'loved', 'unloved' and what their 'potential triggers' might be. An emotionally competent person also knows what it might be like for others to be around them when they are 'happy', 'mad', 'glad', 'sad', 'loved', 'unloved'.

Eurocentric. Thinking that is primarily rooted in 'European Tradition'. Often not much consideration is given as to whether this thinking works across-the board with diverse service users that have roots and heritage from beyond Europe.

Equality of Access. The idea that everyone should have access to the resources and opportunities necessary for a safe and healthy life. This includes people, the expression of ideas, opportunities to develop and progress, and services, to mention just a few.

Exclusion. In this book we are referring to the personal and/or professional consequences for clients and service users when their helpers and other practitioners do not take their advocacy and service user resource roles seriously, or do not prepare for them personally and or professionally, so that clients/service users feel left out at times.

Hate crime. A crime motivated by racial, language, cultural, sexual, or other prejudice, typically involving physical and/or emotional violence.

Inclusion. In this book we are referring to service users being 'welcomed' by practitioners and service providers and for services to be designed around 'a welcoming framework'. For most service users this is expressed as a 'feeling': "...I felt really prepared for by my worker...They took the time to get to know me... They really listened..."

Internalised Racism. When people have been victims of direct and indirect racism and discrimination, such as name calling, stereotyping, low expectations, or bias, they then may start to internalise these feelings and act upon them themselves. This might include seeing themselves and those around them as inferior, acting in a stereotypical manner, and/or having low expectations for those within their colour, culture, or tradition. This could extend to perpetrating violent acts against those with similar roots or appearance.

For many individuals and groups, internalised racism is a challenge for daily living and is often seen as a lot worse than racism itself.

Internalised Sexism. People who have been victims of direct and indirect sexism and sexual harassment – like name calling, stereotyping, low expectations, bias, emotional and physically violent acts – may start to internalise these feelings and act on them. This 'ism' is generally associated with girls and women. Again, victims may see themselves and other females as inferior, start to act in a stereotypical manner, have low expectations for those within their gender, and/or perpetrate bullying, harassment, and low expectations against those of the same gender. Again, internalised sexism is a challenge for daily living and often seen as worse than sexism itself.

Internalised Issues. Sometimes members of marginalised groups hold an 'internalised' view toward their own group that is usually negative and often based upon negative stereotypes and unflattering assumptions. Alternatively, they may start to affirm negative stereotypes of themselves.

Marginalisation. Treatment of a person, group, or concept as insignificant or inferior that places them outside of the mainstream society.

Multiculturalism. The practice of acknowledging and respecting the many cultures, religions, languages, social equality, races, ethnicities, attitudes, and opinions within an environment. Multicultural theory and practice promote peaceful coexistence of all identities, viewpoints, and people.

Chapter Conclusion

This chapter had a lot within it, looking at the types of thoughts and influences that have been the foundation and a basis for this book assumptions. These assumptions, ones that can grow and change over time have their roots in every life experience, religious and cultural participation and include several areas for 'positive thinking for the generation of hope for us all in the now'.

We are off to a good start! Hopefully, any reader confusion (if there is any) will get less as the chapters' progress, we can assure you. Some of our readers could maybe especially find it useful to read any of the book chapters more than just once before moving onto the next and or it may be helpful to even read the final chapter first (and then start from the beginning) some of our past readers have appreciated this and have commented on the flexibility for reading this book and their thoughts and comments could prove of some use to our new readers.

Either way, please take a moment to consider and or reconsider…what do you think about what you have read so far, does it make any sense to you and your life (say in the 'past' or 'during present moments' or maybe even when you think about 'your potential future' experiences)?

Explain:

Does 'the reading' feel 'familiar' to you in any way? Y/N
Explain:

Our lives = our 'lived experiences' (and, or our 'over and under reactions' to them).

Families, and my other relationships even if 'indirect' (maybe to us) such as society, humanity, etc. = 'the us'-collective lived experiences … 'the others'.

This book is, as one of the 'composite focus' group members humorously calls "…another self-help book…" No one owns the expression 'a lived experience', but at times it seems as if certain types of professions, certain types of individuals, and groups to have 'attached' this phrase to themselves and or their professions[20].

This book genuinely seeks out to provide our readers diverse and practical opportunities to get to know more about themselves and others and to provide practical pathways to process this additional life awareness, leading to more hope, and to more joy being added to our own individual lives and our own individual expressions…encouraging us all to 'live more in the now', regardless of our personal circumstances.

In the next chapter, we will be introducing some very interesting 'composite' case study characters, for your consideration and perhaps for you to then compare and contrast to some of their stories to some from your own interesting life experiences and or from the interesting stories of others around you.

---

[20] Counsellors, coaches, social workers, teachers, youth workers, politicians, etc.

Considering Our Own
'Lived Experiences'

For a lot of us, this phrase, 'a lived experience' might be a relatively new one. It is usually associated with issues that we have discussed earlier within this book and also includes;

Childhood Associations

Before going any further, some more 'in-chapter questions' for our readers to ponder:

What are your thoughts about your own 'childhood', has it impacted upon 'how you perceive and react to things inside and around you? Have we often thought about our childhood moments and then consider how (and if) we might have 'described ourselves as being products of these same childhood moments'? If so, is this is very similar to the manner that several Eurocentric psychology analytical theorists tend to say that we do (when trying to 'define and describe the individual')?

For example, *'William'(he/him)* says that he is 'OK', but states that he is very much a product of a dominant mother and a father that had low self-esteem issues since his own childhood.

"…Being a child of the 70s a lot of my friends had families where both parents worked…", but it always seemed that, while his mother held down a full-time job, she also juggled several other areas of her life and interests such as being the lead childcare provider, cook, being in her own clubs and activities e.g., women's choir, took regular college courses, joined a weekend walking group, "…she was always doing something…" and in some ways she was always more active in the community than her children ever were William states.

"…My Dad always worked, and he always tried to squeeze in coming to our school activities where he could. I did not feel unloved or neglected most times but when I read these modern self-help books from my 'middle aged eyes' and see the multiple issues around 'lost men[21]' being discussed in 'bite size chunks' on social media platforms, I guess I could easily empathise with men that might 'feel not connected to anything' and or maybe that do not have many hobbies or are just maybe from the viewpoint of 'standing on the outside' of social relationships and my dad might even be called 'a boring workaholic' …".

William continues to state that in the past recent few years he became a pandemic volunteer, something that he really enjoyed ("…every day is a different one and there is always something very interesting to do…").

---

[21] E.g. being less or non-assertive, not having hobbies, lacking in social skills, limited career risk taker, etc.

"…I made a lot of new friends and took several online CPD courses that I would possibly never have even considered in the past. It was like I watched the world go by in the past.

This is where I first heard the phrase 'a lived experience', especially when it was used for considering those who were either sick and or dying of Covid and or those groups that might have been reluctant to take the Covid-19 vaccine or booster…" I was very surprised by the individuals and communities that are hesitant to taking the Covid-19 vaccine and have been curious about what had happened within their lives to make them feel this way. I do not judge and even though I am very curious, I will always work very hard to stay focused, while supporting those that come through the doors looking to get their Covid tests.

'Janice' (she/her) is in her 30s and described herself as 'a product of society', "…while a lot of women were working and being very busy" as *William* described, "…men and boys they were not regularly sexually assaulted since primary school like I was and like loads of other girls and women around the world were and that still are. I have gotten too use to this sadly ….

I did not have any one to protect me and several people say that I am 'a walking contradiction', because I seem so tough on the outside, but yet so very vulnerable to boys and men from my past.

My lived experience, totally from my point of view grew out of being 'a plaything for men and boys', this led to getting used to not seeing myself and my body at times as my own, and definitely not as a wonderful creation that the universe created for giving to myself and to others as I choose (or maybe not as the case might be) any physical company, intimacy, comfort, and protection.

I had several friends and associates call me 'angry', and 'closed' as a person…yes I would say that my lived experiences often get in the way of 'my now' and definitely gets in the way of me empathising with others about 'their stuff' big time…" "…I am not self-centred; I just do not have the capacity right now to easily take on other people's issues when my wounds standout like a traffic signal…".

'Robert' (he/him), is in his 60s and grew up in San Diego. He states that he knows nothing else but 'race' "…as a kid I had to learn how to fight or I would get my ass kicked every day going to school, could get beat up at school once I got there and get beat up while going home from school. 'Race' was on the news 24/7 and literally within everything that I wanted to enjoy it seemed as well… in sports, in music …my parents even went to every social protest going in the 60s it seemed. Sometimes they took us along too…being a curious kid, where I was afraid at times, I found them strangely enjoyable at times.

When playing sports, I remember that I tended to mainly be 'chosen' by the Hispanic or Black kids. I also self-selected myself into these groups when I had a choice too, I guess.

Ironically, in my family we knew more about 'the Kennedy brothers', other white liberals and progressives than most white people did back in the day… you figure that out. As a young person, you could say that me and my siblings knew a lot about the various political candidates, the local candidates and the national ones too. My parents always voted for the 'Democrats'. They would be turning over in their graves had they heard about Trump.

I have always been described as 'having a chip on my shoulder' and every time I heard that sentence I always said, "…yes, and so what?"

'Dorothea' (She/Her)

"…my childhood was all about my colour to me, nothing else really mattered than that…I was always a darker skin tone than any group of people that I was with…always, even when with my family. I am not aware how I got this way; I just was. My parents and grandparents on both sides were not dark. Adults always described me as 'very pretty', especially when compared to other children that were around me. To the other children, my name was 'Dora the dark princess'…I hated most of the children around me although I never told them that or I never even tried to beat any one up even though I probably could.

For many years this really hurt me, and I hated going to school and, often found any excuse not to go. My father, bless him he allowed me to live with his brother in Birmingham from the age of 10 because he could never handle the fact that I was being teased or that I was so very unhappy back then. I was so relieved, in Birmingham there were several 'shades' around me and I did not feel so out of place and alone. I even had a best friend named *'Anu'*, and we got on like a house on fire…

I am 47 now and look back upon my childhood and I go then always between blaming my parents for not protecting me enough and then to society for being so racist and so bias against people that looked very different than the little blond hair blue eyed girls and big women that they seem to flag up in the movies and in the magazines…

When I started to look at 'boys', it seemed like a lot of them seem to have a 'main friendship group' that looked a lot like them and there were some that seem to only attract white girls…these weren't not the type of children that wanted to be my friend…my uncle had loads of lady friends that tried their best to make me look pretty, they brought me clothes, took me to the salon, and even helped me to stay quite slim through exercise and calorie reduction…I think some boys and even some girls were around and being were nice to me because they thought I look like a fashion model…you would not be surprised that I ended up in the fashion field, they seemed to accept me here, although mainly older white men tried to pursue me romantically."

'Anu' (She/Her) 48, while very close to *Dorothea* growing up, some of her key 'childhood moments' were very different to her. "…*Dorothea* always seemed to attract a lot a people and everyone wanted to be her friend. She was very pretty although if you spoke to her, she always said the same thing, that she hated her darker skin and wished that she was much lighter skin and wanted to live somewhere a long was away from Birmingham. I was in a wheelchair since the age of six due to a car accident and as a child I had to have my school mates push me around or had to simply wait until an adult came around to push my chair. Sometimes I had to wait a long time. When *Dorothea* joined our school, she would never let anyone push my chair only her.

"…I only felt out of place until I met *Dorothea*…we did everything together and we are very close now as adults. I did not have many friends, even though at my school, it was a 'policy', we all had to be friends with everybody. I did not even have a boyfriend until my second year of university.

I have an electric chair now and still have to remind Dorothea of this fact now, when we see each other, she rushes straight to push my electric chair.

I am lucky that my family accepted her, they did as if she was just another one of their daughters. My family is Muslim and she was Christian and we seemed like 'one big happy family'..." ...I am sure they were just pleased that I had a very best friend.me too!..." I would not describe myself as an 'angry child, my accident was just that, an accident...".

Just to remind our readers, *'William'*, *'Janice'*, *'Robert'*, *'Dorothea' and 'Anu'* are just fictional names arising from real stories and events described to us over several years.

From watching modern television and or other social media formats like Facebook you would have regularly seen and heard the phrase, 'a lived experience' being connected to perhaps an individual's experience of poverty, maybe even the experiences of people living with depression and/or bipolar conditions, maybe from those that were care givers, and or from those with other mental and emotional health challenges, maybe even those that have been involved with the criminal justice system, etc..

The potential experiences that human beings wake up to and react to and or not react to and or maybe that 'others' react to, these are vast and possibly even very confusing and 'potentially unseen' to those looking on.

Chapter Conclusion

One of the key takeaways from this chapter is for you or anyone of us, even though it may seem emotionally and or intellectually difficult at times, but in our own way to *begin to consider and or reconsider if some of your own lived experiences might have had an impact, this can be very insightful and very life enhancing. This can also be true when reflecting upon our childhood moments...potentially painful at time, but hopefully leading to enlightenment and inner peace.*

So far...e.g. what about your own 'awake <u>thinking</u>' and or your own 'awake <u>actions</u>, and or your own awake <u>reactions</u> and or awake <u>expressions</u>'? **Note: Often people see this type of question as generating 'confidential thoughts', please only write your reflections for your personal[22] viewing only.**

Note: Topics from this chapter specifically might bring up issues for some readers, these might relate to feelings connected to and ranging from moments and experiences that could have been based upon happiness, sadness, anger, trauma, lack of confidence, low self-esteem, etc. <u>It is important to have positive and healthy support systems to call upon if needed</u>.

Some readers from earlier versions of this book have described this chapter as being personally enlightening and

---

[22] Of course, please feel free to share as you feel comfortable to do so.

one even described it "...as like a weight was lifted off of my shoulders..."

In the next chapter we look at the term and expression of 'gender' and consider where and how it potentially might fit into the discussions for a lived experience and explore what impact it might have had upon us all.

Feel free to take a 'pause' in your reading if there is a need for further personal reflection, meditation, exercise, a walk, a dance, a nice snack, etc...you choose!

Some Considerations of 'Gender'

When it comes to the term 'gender' most of us only see two sexes, one 'male' and one 'female', especially when considered with reference to social and cultural differences rather than biological ones.

What happens when there are individuals, families, communities, local, regional, and national governments (for example) and institutional frameworks that might have rules and legislations that have and continue to have an influence upon how we might see and wish to express our lives? Does this and or can this potentially impact how 'gender' is expressed within our communities? Y/N Explain:

This book does not even pretend to be an expert on 'gender' as it could relate to defining and or illustrating exact examples of 'a lived experience'. On the contrary, we suppose this is another area where an individual life experience(s) can be considered unique, but then not to be 'gender compared and our contrasted' to anyone else's view and or definitions of the term 'gender'.

What if however, rather than us trying to be so clever and thinking that we can just understand any and all of those around us, why not simply, as 'a starting point' just listen, yes just listen to individuals and simply accept stories here, from 'the story tellers', as if they were 'experts of their own lives'.

'Sean' ('they/them') describes themselves as a 32-year-old 'soul crazy freak'. *Sean* says that their life experience is not unique and that they have more in common with the majority of people around them…just struggling to make a living and looking for nice people to share some good times with.

But when they tell you more about their life, while they are very interesting and unique story tellers, their relationships of any kind were often quite described as intense and unfortunate at times…people always had opinion about 'people like me', yet not knowing anything about me.

Sean's birth certificate describes them as a 'male', but although sexually attracted to both men and women, which made them popular at times (they described this with a smile), *Sean* from a very young age wanted to be called 'a person' and dress as they pleased and not as society says a boy or girl should look like… "… I don't think I had it bad as some, my family loved me and I loved them, although I think we all assumed that we were/are too hard on each other.

I feel often 'judging' of other people and I am always wanting to know what makes them 'tick'.

I think some of us are confused and regularly put our confusion onto our families, friends and our co-workers at times. Facebook, Instagram, and other social media platforms totally add to the mess. I think people that get me will enjoy and respect me more than those that don't.

People seem to always make assumptions about me, the most popular one is that my parents screwed me up when I was 'little' and this explains my personality…"

'Tetnya' (they/them) talks very 'differently' to *Sean*, while *Sean* was curious about other people, *Tetnya* states they could go the rest of their life being left alone. "…I am old enough to remember being beaten up as a young person because of who and how I was. I had learned how to do well in school as a way of 'self-protection' and kept my hopes and wishes to myself. I was not always clear about how and who I was, so how was I supposed to be assertive or preachy to others about who they should be.

I am a bit private, basically go to work and go home. People at my work places soon find out that I am 'somewhat open', but I do not tolerate any gossip about me and my lifestyle. If anyone wants to know something about me, all they have to do is ask, I will either answer them or I won't. I have even left jobs if I felt that others around me were gossiping about me…sometime our own kind are the worst at gossiping…".

Do you remember *'William'*, he says that 'being a man was not a choice' and if he could do it all over again, that he might do it all over again as a 'woman', "…could not hurt…" It always seemed that society was always showing girls as being soft and good and boys being foolish and not so much 'common sense'. I am almost 100% sure that 'my lived experience story' would be drastically different had I been a woman, for one I would definitely have had more positive role models and society would have given me much more of 'a nudge' than they have in my life as *'William'*.

Does 'Gender' really matter (with regard to considering someone's lived experiences)? Explain:

Does 'gender' matter within your own lived experience? Y/N

Some interesting terms and phrases to consider and discuss:

People of colour. A term used to describe all non-white racial and ethnic groups.

Social Construct. An idea that appears to be natural and obvious to those who accept it, but may or may not represent reality.

Social Justice. The fair and just relationships between the individual and society, where all people have a right to fair and equitable treatment, support, and resources.

Tolerance. In this instance we are referring to the ability and willingness of practitioners, supervisors, training providers, service users, and other stakeholders to tolerate counselling and psychological theories, opinions, and behaviours that we may personally, professionally, or collectively dislike or disagree with.

Here we are aiming toward a helper-service user relationship that is based on open mindedness, lack of bias, and sustainable mutual respect; a relationship that can express its full creative potential.

Transgender is often a term that could include the diverse ways that some individual's persons self-perceived identity for the term 'gender'.

Often this can be different to the gender listed on their birth certificate.

It is always best to use language that individuals use for themselves.

White. In the UK, many organisations that use an 'ethnic monitoring form' often use the term 'White British'. In this instance they are referring to those individuals who have their roots and origins within the British Isles. In some instances, it includes those who have indicated their race as 'White', such as Irish, French, German, Italian, Lebanese, Arab, or Caucasian.

It is important to note that 'White' is not a 'scientific' and or 'anthropological' term or designation, although it is generally accepted and widely used around the world.

Chapter Conclusion

As we can all hopefully see, when considering 'gender' like most things to do with global beings, discussions are not always straight forward and often expressed as 'fluid' with regard to this topic. In saying that, in hearing from our 'case studies', to them their lived experiences are sometimes related to 'their self-described gender', and or 'the general society definitions', related to gender but not totally defined by either one.

Words and phrases to describe ourselves can often be very constricting and limited, where it does not usually give us much space to be an individual global being. I have always thought it was important to let people 'self-describe themselves'. When we let this happen, there is usually 'an interesting story' [23]behind how we may and or may not describe ourselves.

We have included some of these 'self-descriptions' below as an illustration of how language can shape how we see ourselves and how others may view us.

Examples of 'gender neutral language' for everyday life:

- Aunt/uncle changed **to** 'pibling' (stands for "parent's sibling)
- boyfriend/husband or girlfriend/wife changed **to** 'partner and or significant other'
- buddy/mate changed **to** 'friend'
- granddaughter/grandson changed **to** 'grandchild'
- grandma / grandpa changed **to** 'grandparent'
- husband or wife changed **to** 'spouse'
- mother or father changed **to** 'parent'
- sister or brother changed **to** 'sibling'
- son or daughter changed **to** 'child or progeny'
- girl or boy changed **to** 'young person', 'kid', or 'teen' handsome or beautiful changed **to** 'attractive' or 'good-looking', human to 'person' or 'being' woman or man changed **to** 'adult'
- *any term/phrase that uses the 'man' or 'woman' at the end* **can simply be changed to make it 'person' centred and then 'gender neutral'.**

---

[23] Remember our friends *William, Janice, Robert, Sean, Dorothea and Anu?*

Could you imagine using gender neutral terms and phrases in your everyday communication, especially if it has a positive impact upon those that you love and or support and or work with? Y/ N Explain:

In the next chapter we will explore[24] if our own lived experiences have helped and or hindered us at different times in our lives.

---

[24] 'Individually considered' but discussed within a 'supportive group setting'.

Self-Assessing How and If Your Learned Experiences Have Helped or Hindered You Thus Far?

Introduction

The phases of 'the process' or 'the journey', at least from this author's point view revolves around you considering if it felt like you have lost something[25] (or not) from your lived experience(s), say from your increasing self-awareness point of view (either from 'the living and experiencing' and or from the actual 'self-reflection' of your lived experiences).

Practically speaking, some would say that "...if you haven't lost anything, then what's the problem? ..." 'Robert' (He/Him)

---

[25] In terms of 'loss', we are referring to areas in life such as pride, lifestyle, friendships and or a significant other, work, potential work, hope, joy, energy, peace of mind, mental health, well-being, respect(generally), respect for others, self-esteem, self-image, health, positive outlook,

When hearing from *William*, "…I think that I was 'a mixed bag', I seemed to have been attracted to attractive women that easily could and do look after themselves but at the same time if I am honest, I sometimes then resented that they seemed to not really have needed me and it seems like they always led a very active social and hobby life…I have been married three times and I have no problems with stating that 'my so called lived experience' has left me feeling very 'wounded', for myself and for others around me that I may have regularly taken for granted and or the many many others that I might have unfairly projected too much of my own crap upon…I am very sorry…"

William self-described his lived experiences, of his own feelings revolving around feeling that he had a 'loss of positive male role model' in his father and a 'loss' from having a mother that seem to care more about her own well-being, fun and career development more than the well-being of her own children (such as encouraging them with following in her footsteps and with the development of their own individual well-being to a high level as well).

From the limited information that you have been provided about *William* so far, do you agree with his own views and his own self-reflections about, say his own expressed lived experiences? Y/N Explain.

One focus group strongly felt that 'men', especially 'white men had been 'feeling lost' (e.g. specifically, when compared to women) since at least the various world wars when women were generally expected to help with war efforts, this while still expected to raise and look after their children and their households. The focus group stated that this was more of an example of a societal issue, one that was 'never really talked about' (in schools and or within families for example) and that *William's* parents and grandparent's own lived experiences were passed down through 'the family' but were never actually communicated nor were the problematic views on men and women ever 'interrupted' or 'challenged'. The focus group also felt that it was good that he had no children at present because his 'long line of unchecked lived experiences' would definitely have impacted upon his children and their relationships (within themselves individually, within a family setting, within their friends and associates, as teenagers, as adults, etc).

Janice

Janice has expressed her self-reflections as "...it's amazing that before we agreed to start this focus group, I did not think that I had anything 'in common' with most people generally, and I at least I had assumed that no one ever really talked about certain things like this (chronic sexual assaults from childhood to adulthood)." "...I am similar to *William*, I am wounded and have lost many friends and potential friends because they felt that I was either too guarded , or very much too angry...this was very much though listening to me, even when considering if it[26] had helped me (which it did)...I am a survivor that has learned a lot about herself but definitely wish

---

[26] My own reflections of my own lived experiences.

I could have had a life without sexual assaults…I had boys and men that I really liked but sex, sexual assaults, these areas usually killed off any chance of forming any healthy relationship…"

From the limited information that you have been provided about *William* so far, do you agree with his own views and his own self-reflections about, say his own expressed lived experiences? Y/N Explain.

What do you think about *Janice* from the limited information that you have read so far? Explain.

Finally, we have *Robert*, I am very sure that our readers assumed that this man was 'a person of colour' , this honestly was not the case. Robert was adopted by what he describes as a very loving Hispanic family and growing up in a '…primarily working-class area…' of San Diego (California). When you get to know Robert, he'll tell you himself that at times he felt very guilty when others in his family got teased at times during his childhood and he didn't. Even when discussing his experience(s) with the criminal justice system, this area was one area that was drastically different than his brothers and cousins. …there was even a time when I was arrested as a teenager along with some of his other Hispanic childhood friends, but the police let me go within minutes once I stated that "…I am just an adopted 'white boy'…"

"…My lived experiences were confusing to me at most times, I was 'privileged' and treated very differently than the rest of the family. My family treated me as a proud Hispanic boy with Irish roots, it took me years to see that my life was not a hindrance and that even now I genuinely think that…even blessed moments… can have 'bumps and bruises' at times. Even now I must correct other people's assumptions that growing up in a 'dual heritage family' would somehow screw me up for life.

My main lived experiences, if I am honest stem from my experiences related to losing my parents in a car accident when I was in my mid 20s and still trying to figure things out after that. I felt this was more of a struggle for me personally than 'race' ever was.

I had friends and partners from a variety of races and cultures and people seem to find it easy to be around me. Because of this I think led to me becoming a community nurse practitioner and to having my office only 10 minutes from where I was raised…how's that for a lived life irony? …"

What do you think about Robert's life and his 'self-discovery insights' from what you have read so far?

Most of the two focus groups felt that *Robert's* lived experiences where shaped by the people around him, and those like them who might have made several regular assumptions along the way, some (assumptions) that *Robert* too had unfairly took ownership of at times during his own admission.

Dorothea states that her life meant that she wasted a lot of time not knowing the beauty of being black, of being part of the black and brown community (even when in white majority area) ,especially the joys of being a black woman. People say we have 'super powers', yes now I truly know what they meant.

There were many people of colour that could have been a 'gift' to me and me to them. I predominately dated white men. Upon reflection, men of colour were 'interested' also I was naive about them and their intentions…mainly because I had no experience of them. My current partner always says that he worries that I will leave him for a black man…he may be right.

Anu says that living in a wheel chair helped to develop her 'empath spirit', which she says this in turn helped her to show the appreciation for her many gifts and talents.

Anu states that her life experiences led her to running for the local council, something that she enjoyed for the past 11 years.

Some interesting terms and phrases to consider and discuss:

Self- Disclosure. Voluntarily sharing (a disclosure) some information about yourself, perhaps something that you do not normally let others know. Sometimes in a work and or voluntary work setting, there are occasions where certain areas of your life where it might be made 'mandatory' to share information such as your financial details, your previous convictions, your legal cautions, your drug and alcohol history, other diversity details[27],etc.

Self-Defined. A moment and or situation where you might explain in your own way, without pressure maybe 'who' you are, 'how' you are and 'why' (your rationale) you are doing something and or why you have certain thoughts

---

[27] Marital status, religion, sexuality preference, gender at birth, stated learning and or medical status, age, etc.

and or views. Often because of 'time constraints', individuals are not given the opportunity to fully explain their full range of thoughts and experiences and then a 'tick box' form is 'the preferred choice' for gathering the views, preferences and interests of global beings.

Chapter Conclusion

Considering what parts of our lives helped and or hindered us…wow, not an easy learning opportunity for most of us to tackle, regardless of age and or the circumstances.

A lot of our thinking and 'weighing up of the range of choices that could be available to us for self-reflection and 'critical self-examinations', these aren't easily just 'self-defined' as can be said about other 'personal self-esteem and self-image' issues, but these two consideration areas(such as defining what has 'helped' and or 'hindered' us, etc) are nowadays often 'defined by external sources' such as social media, television , news media, our peer groups, our family, our helping professionals, etc. *Can you think of anymore external sources that often 'define us'?*

Thinking back to what *William, Janice, Robert, Sean, Dorothea and Anu* (along with the various focus groups) mentioned within their diverse comments and self-reflective experiences and views, maybe even *when thinking about some of your own lived experiences …which ones 'helped' or 'hindered' you? Explain.* In certain situations, there are some that would say "…just stop your moaning and get on with things…", and perhaps, while if you adopt this stance, by maybe not 'being positive' about your lived experiences, you aren't 'being negative' about it either…I wonder? *What do you think about the latter sentence?*

The next chapter will explore what we want 'others' (friends, families, allies, etc.) to know about us, especially the 'helpers'.

What Do You Want Others to Know About You?

Introduction

Going back to our spoken word artists and slam poetry artists friends, they say things like;

- "…sharing my stories is like 'taking in a breath of air…sometimes it is fresh air' going into me and out of me…sometimes it was 'polluted air' coming in and going out of me."
- Often people [28]will create 'a narrative' about others' lives, especially if we have not yet 'staked our own claim' about who we really are ourselves.
- Know that we are 'individuals and not a clone', one that can't easily be 'sized up' within just in a few minutes.
- I may have expressed a range of emotions in front of you and others, but these should not keep

---

[28] Including social media, etc.

defining me, I am an individual, one that grows and changes daily.

- Sometimes I might 'confuse myself'.

- you, your thoughts, and experiences should be accessible to me too, especially if you wish to know me, support me, support my family, support my friends and support my communities...

> *What do you think about the comments above...do any of them resonate with you? Y/N Explain:*

In doing a recent weekend thought shower exercise, several of the participants completed a 'lived experience' exercise, but along the way kept talking to those inside and outside of their small groups. The topic seemed a very interesting one.

Their 'discussions' seemed to fall into three main 'discussions points':

Stereotypes and Fantasies

For a lot of things in 'life' and to a lot of us, "... 'there is no smoke without fire'..."

Continuing on, with this thinking, for a lot of us if we see and or hear about certain behaviours, actions and attitudes by individuals, families, groups and communities, even though it definitely isn't 'politically correct thinking', we might make a mental note (assumptions) to ourselves maybe something like this "... see I told you, they really are like this, put them in certain situations and 'they revert back to type' (the 'stereotypical images)…".

Trying to explain this phenomenon can be very complicated and is definitely wrapped up within several layer of social and anthropological considerations and discussions, this book would be several hundred pages longer if it tried to tackle this point in a very comprehensive manner.

A 'shorter answer', one that still has some relevance, might be connected to the words and terms like 'survival', 'learned habits', etc., where since the early recordings of global beings, a lot of populations copied each other, especially if it could lead to more food…to more power… and to a higher sense of esteem and or legacy.

Like with most stereotypes and fantasies, there is usually 'a story behind them' and not connected to intellectual prowess and or the size of one's brains. 'This story' often if drilled down can usually be related to 'survival and imitation'.

It is important to not be afraid to 'look behind political correctness filters' and respectfully ask individuals what's really on yours or their mind;
- *"…Why do you do that? …"*
- *"…Where did you learn how to do that? …"*
- *"…Are you aware of when you might be straying into what might be called 'stereotypical behaviour'? …"*
Explain:

Limitations

One of the clear messages that have ran throughout this book, including during its early planning and development stages was that a lot of us do not like 'being pigeon holed', and or 'being labelled as a 'type'.

Where a lot of self-help and personal development movements going back thousands of years, most of these introduced the notion, very much in their own particular ways that *anything is possible, especially when 'linked to intention'* and some introduced various forms of 'rituals and practices to help get you there' (readings, chanting, practicing, studying, rehearsing, meditating, reflecting, moving, honouring, dancing, travelling, listening, playing, etc).

Often with our consideration of the phrase 'a lived experience', this can even with good intentions, lead to us just only seeing global beings by what they potentially can't do and or potentially seeing them as somehow 'being flawed just by their waking up' this morning[29] .

Example:

Certain lived experiences will mean that certain life aims and expectations[30] might not be able to happen, say when compared to those without these "…certain…" type of lived experience…in this example we could use learning disabilities, and or long-term medical challenge, etc). I would strongly suggest that you make diverse friends and associates with learning challenges, medical challenges and other type life experiences, if you are open, committed, and really trying to 'be with them' (as opposed to just 'looking in' from the

---

[29] e.g. in 'certain areas', with having the parents that we do, by the friends and associates that we have/have had, by our learning styles and challenges, etc.

[30] All 'self-defined'.

outside), you will see as generations of us have, *hope and joy can reside anywhere*!

Some within our focus group have listed their lived experiences 'limiters' as (listed in no particular order):

- age
- physical challenges
- mental challenges
- criminal record
- children
- no money
- being homeless
- race
- colour
- class
- language
- size
- job level
- gender
- learning styles
- being jobless

What 'helpers' really need to know

Global being individuals (and groups that they belong to) often seem to want a variety of things such as:

- ✓ To be seen and heard as individuals (and at times, as a 'respectful collection of individuals').
- ✓ That even when you might 'see me/us' do some of the most self-destructive things and or the most

confusing things to myself, to you and around you, please do try to look past this, even while difficult to see me...see us!

✓ Just because you might be romantically involved/might have been romantically involved with someone that looks like me, that doesn't mean that you know me and or that I am the same as 'your past' experiences of people that look like me.

✓ *I want to know about you and your intentions too...for someone like me...for the work that you do...and for what gets you up in the morning?*

Chapter Conclusion

We all make assumptions and show certain bias at times, this is part of being global beings.

Hopefully as you have begun to see (and or potentially reconsider a bit further in yours and others lives) is that while 'stereotypes', 'myths' and fantasies seem to be 'politically incorrect words and phrases' most times, for a lot of us, these are areas that are worth exploring rather than just keeping in your heads or hearts and or acting upon them behind closed doors (in your decision making, in your marketing materials, in your grant bids, etc) ... the roots of most bias (racial, sexual, gender, religious, etc.) often began with stereotypes, so *potentially asking honest, direct questions, within a respectful manner may lead to a very positive and 'bridge building moment' between individuals, families and their communities and the reduction of bias.*

Often non-verbal methods such as meditation, reflection, prayer, engaging in 'positive communication games', etc. these *can lead to* the same destination and with *rarely anyone getting their feelings hurt and or having problems with any serious misunderstandings developing... these areas are often 'hard to walk back' so always please be very clear in your intentions and be very clear with any follow-on communicational strategies.*

In 'people to people' work, being 'open' to share about yourself is crucial to building good relationships with those you are trying to support.

'A very positive diversity and inclusion ready' supervisor and or mentor would prove very useful here too. I am not aware of any modern and 'inclusion looking' organisation that does not see the added value of 'positive self-disclosure'.

The next chapter explores what is left to do to explore within solution focused frameworks, how to make the best of our 'lived experience, personal insights, and new self-realisations'.

Self-Assessment: What is There Still Left for You to Do (With Regard to Your Own Lived Experiences)

When we check back in with *Michael, Janice, Robert, Dorothea and Anu they make self-suggestion areas such as:*

Michael

"…I need to get out of my own head at times. I know I could do a lot more for my own personal development without only comparing myself to my parents. Along with my pandemic volunteer work, I have also joined a 'Men's Identity Group', we speak and consider about so many things as 'men', we go very deep at times…I am working on my self-image and have been 'experimenting' with what life has to offer within my current CPD activities and developing new hobbies, alone and with some of the group members…new friends.

I am very pleased with taking part in this focus group and for taking the time to develop myself in the company of my new friends.

I never thought that I would get to know about my lived experience…just thinking that it was my destiny to have more bad luck than other people. I am more optimistic and hopeful than even. I hope my lived experience will even expand more in the future, where I can engage with my elderly parents differently than I have in my younger years…it could not hurt…".

Janice

"…I still need to unpack several layers of trauma from my life experiences. There are countries and cultures that come through wars, natural disasters, major civil unrest and amazingly they are still able to rebuild, still develop their family and their culture…I want to be more like them…surviving to live, love and add to society. I am not saying that I am perfect and, that I still won't piss people off along the way or still not be very sad or angry at times, but I am now living my best life much better than I did in the past.

Blaming others only limited my own narratives, my lived experience story, things that I guess I so easily gave it away to boys and men. I know Duncan might say that I am close to blaming others but to me I am really not (I think), more of a 'loss' really, I could have and still could have men, but more as allies and maybe my approach and my attitude is what can now make the difference…"

Robert

"…I need to stop apologising for my contradictory views about 'life' and just learn to live my own self-actualised life.

There are so many things that I could be missing out on by the over-examining my life and my past choices.

I wish my parents were alive, would definitely would have loved to have had discussions about their lives, their lived experiences. I think this would be terrific. I would also let them know my gratitude for them adopting me and how my lived experience would have had a great loss if I was not their son and if they weren't my parents…".

Tetnya

"…I am ok with living as an 'introvert', not a 'hermit' though, these are two different things. I have come to realise it is not that I see others as always difficult to live with and around, it is that I don't always have the confidence to feel worthy enough at times around others.

This is the most that I have ever shared with other people, it was not as bad as I thought, although I can't guarantee that I will ever do it again anytime soon…".

Sean

"…I need to stop hiding so much behind everything and just be me and be alright that my views of myself are 'fluid', but still mine. Other people can live their own lived experiences with no further judgments from me, at least that is one thing that I can say that I will do and mean it. Doing this has added nothing to my own life I think and in a lot of cases I often expected others to 'prove me wrong' about my assumptions of them. It is not easy to be so honest now. Maybe I need 'another go' with the focus group.

I am more than just sex or my gender. Sure, I like being physically intimate, but there is so much more to me than get tied in knots, especially about how I should describe myself, I am just as fluid as my lifestyle or not…at least my lived experience story will be a great read to somebody, I hope!…".

Dorothea

"…I need to just try to live my best life and not hurt anyone…I am so curious about so many things connected to race and men. With me being such 'a late bloomer' others have possibly experienced much more than I have, in some ways I guess you can even say that I am immature.

Not to sound too naive, but learning about my lived experience, gives me hope for the future and that my possibilities and the possibilities of my family are not written in stone or 'predestined'. 'Living in the now' is something I never really thought about…seemed like a religious thing at first, but trying to make sense of my life is more than that. Understanding that others need to have their lives shown more and respected too and not just be a 'me me me' society…"

Anu

"…I want children, the doctors say it might be difficult to go through natural labour birth and that I should consider adoption. Because of my work, I need to consider if I can be a good mother and be a politician…a lot to think about.

I think I have been living a 'quiet version' of my life for too long. Even a politician can be lonely and timid. Love, travel and who knows what is still out there to have new chapters in my lived experiences, yes, I am very hopeful too. I think I have been very good with trying to empathise with the stories and the lived experiences of others so looking at me and developing a more well-rounded lived experience about me should be very doable."

Some Interesting Terms and Phrases to Consider and Discuss:

Bias. When we have conscious and or unconscious thoughts or prejudice for others (individually and or about a group) and or against others (individually and or about a group) that results in them being treated unfairly by you and or by those around you.

This could also include 'actions' such as having positive thoughts, having negative thoughts, having limited and or having stereotypical and or discriminatory thoughts, etc..

White Male Privilege. White male privilege is usually associated with the phrase, 'white privilege ', where a racial group in society (in this instance we are referring to 'white people') is granted 'benefits' within this same society by virtue of being born with a certain skin colour and not by having to earn it. In a lot of case, some within this group are not even aware that that they have access to these benefits and there are some still that are quite naive and do not realise that not everyone has access to these benefits and or types of power.

With roots in European colonialism, imperialism, and the Atlantic slave trade, white privilege has developed in circumstances that have broadly sought to protect white racial privileges, various national citizenships, and other rights or special benefits.

With regard to white men, some within positions of power within society, sometime use their powers in an unfair manner, often therefore creating a disproportionate number of victims which usually include women and non-white groups of people.

White men in position of privilege have and do at times create life and soul-destroying situations for others and then seem as to have no consequence afterwards for their behaviours, nor an intention to make things right.

Self- Care. Self-care generally is considered the practice of consciously doing things that will sustain or improve your mental or physical health. This phrase can be attributed to any one of us and engaging in it can drastically make a positive impact upon someone's overall well-being.

Examples of self-care could include sleeping well, eating healthy food, exercising regularly, having a dedicated meditation programme, being involved in regular programmes that will enhance your mental and emotional awareness, etc.[1]

Chapter Conclusion

Often people feel that they can tell too much about themselves to others (especially to 'the helpers') and then after a while wish that they hadn't said anything at all…some are then even left feeling very vulnerable and exposed afterwards.

There are some of us that believe the letting others share something about themselves without you doing the same thing, that this can be tricky situation, one that can work out very very well (and move 'the helping process' along) or turn out very badly indeed (where the communication process can feel quite fragile), due to a power imbalance that went array.

This can be especially true when you genuinely wanted to come across as 'equal to your client/service user', where your own global being lived experiences and existence did not simply disappear just because you may have a paid or unpaid role to assist and or support them.

Hopefully our readers have begun to realise, that we all have' a lived experience' by virtue of being global beings and that while yours will always be yours (and mine will always be mine), at the same time it potentially always stand the risk for being open to be misunderstood, culturally misappropriated for diverse intentions, and potentially have a high chance of a good result when 'power' (the equal sharing of hopes , needs and intentions) is 'by design' is not misused between the helper and helpee.

Even though we have tried to gradually integrate the theme within each chapter, the importance of taking ownership of 'our own lived experiences' (regardless of whether we see certain m moments from them as being positive and or maybe less than positive) and that for Global beings (regardless of race, creed, culture, class, learning styles, learning difficulties, physical and medical challenges, etc.) this can be a very difficult and complicated process to do, to be part of. Have your views changed and or further developed since starting this book?

Yes/ No Explain:

The final chapter looks at how to reduce bias, prejudging and limited thinking especially when we do not really know much about others.

A Professional Approach: –
'Good Practicing' Out Bias

> Are you or have you ever been a product of 'bias'? Y/N
> Explain:

There are some in society that think that 'bias' is one of the worst things that can hold back large number within our society and that 'bias' can have the most 'victims' of it and that 'the victims' might never even know that it is actually happening to them 'in the moment' and often only becomes clear once a related reflective moment arises (such as might occur within an investigation, employment coaching, therapy, someone confesses to them, etc).

'Bias' itself can be helpful in certain situations and can be carried out with very good intentions, for example especially when you are trying to bring up certain 'marginalised' individuals into 'the mainstream power', so as part of developing a more inclusive society for example you might 'target' those that you think 'might need a break' within society and or maybe just focus on those members in society that disproportionately could be missing out within the workplace and employability populations. In both example areas described above, organisations and their staff are the ones that are openly and at times 'covertly' carrying out the bias 'by design'.

In a lot of cases however, bias is often specifically used to make certain individuals, groups, cultures, residential area residents, users of a community and or institution service(s)[31], to be treated 'negatively and unfairly', while some individuals and groups being treated in a more 'favourable' manner than others, although more often than not they might each be in the same exact situation, and in the 'exact same starting points'. In these cases, for example, maybe those with a limited incomes are regularly and 'unofficially' being excluded or passed over when trying to apply to certain types of housing initiatives. There are several daily real-life examples where community members, citizens of all creeds and cultures, etc. are subject to unfair episodes of bias subjected usually by individuals that they probably do not even know and will never ever get to meet.

With anti-discriminatory practices being the 'gold standard' for most workplaces and 'service organisations', the goal ideally is to have all service users to be able to have equal access to a programme's 'resources[32]'. This is easier said than done however.

Some of the 'roadblocks' and things that can get in the way of service users getting a fair deal in these types of situations could include;

---

[31] This could include health, education, welfare, law, financial institutions, etc.

[32] This could include staffing, employability schemes, etc.

- Staff/helper immaturity and limited self-awareness
- Service users with current immaturity and current limited self-awareness
- Service users with limited allies and or support systems.
- Programmes with unclear intentions
- Limited diversity and inclusion readiness within staff/helper teams
- Limited commitment to anti-discriminatory practices within staff/helper teams
- Staff that play favouritism
- Limited resources
- Resources only targeted at 'certain lived experiences'
- Organisations whose 'marketing strategies' that currently targets those from a certain language and or dialect.
- Programme that only covers those from a certain area and or post codes
- Programme services and opening hours that could exclude certain potential users such as parents, students, and carers

Some bias activity is 'unconscious', where the staff and their programmes may not yet realise what they have done and or have no clue that they have and or otherwise will go onto show any bias such as against those areas listed above and many more real and practical life areas. In this day and age however, with the range of free and low-cost diversity and inclusion CPD programmes available to staff teams, this area (anti-bias strategies) really should be a strong one for most paid and volunteer staff teams.

There has been great number of research and action research programmes completed over several decades within the UK,US,EU and beyond that covers the 'topic of bias', often as part of diversity and inclusion studies and sometimes triggered by a lawsuit(s). The most 'popular areas' where bias can be prevalent are often within 'societal institutions' such as education, welfare, social services, law, politics, etc. include [33]:

- Gender bias
- Parenting/single parent bias
- Sexuality bias
- Colour bias
- Age bias
- Learning style bias
- Parent bias
- Single person bias
- Physical, visual and hearing bias
- Lifestyle bias
- Unmarried family bias
- Language bias
- Housing/residential bias
- Legal system history bias
- Class bias
- 'political bias'
- Academic bias

---

[33] Listed in no particular order.

- Size bias
- Conversational bias
- Food/menu bias
- 'Able body' bias
- those that file complaints being treated 'differently' bias

Then there is 'conscious bias', when you knowingly treat groups and individuals more unfavourably than others. How this shows itself in your everyday relationships and work is very similar to the list above.

This also shows itself in situations such as:

- When only certain types of individuals and groups attend social events
- Low programme take up by certain members and groups from within society
- More interpersonal difficulties between certain types of staff (often based upon gender, skin colour, age, learning styles, culture, religion, etc.)
- More service user and or staff complaints (often based upon gender, skin colour, age, learning styles, culture, religion, etc.)
- More service users-service user conflicts (often based upon gender, skin colour, age, learning styles, culture, religion, etc.)
- Staff turnover at a higher-than-normal rate (often based upon gender, skin colour, age, learning styles, culture, religion, etc.)
- Inconsistent 'service user results'

> Are you aware of any 'conscious and or unconscious bias' that you have personally initiated[34] and or 'conscious and or unconscious bias' that may show itself at your paid/unpaid workplace that is initiated by others. Y/ N Explain: **Note:** we are not trying to look down on any organisations or 'stir things up', especially with any valued charity organisation and or any other valued service provider. On the contrary, it is hoped that our readers and or any volunteers and or any staff will 'cascade' any learning from this book/this CPD programme back to their organisation.

We are all responsible for bias[35] and we all can go a long way to reduce it in schools, within the workplace, within our institutions and within the wider society.

As mentioned earlier, **not all bias is bad or even has a negative intention.** Clearly some bias has and continues to be very damaging to the fabric of a positive community's development unless it can courageously be 'named' and followed up by anti-bias strategies ones that have been carefully developed and put in its place, with timely and sustained monitoring processes that will be implemented alongside.

---

[34] And or have taken a part in.

[35] CEOs, paid and unpaid staff, volunteers, politicians, unions, charities, individuals, families, clergy, elders,

'Bias' is an area that could be reviewed regularly and carefully.

The volunteer programme that follows this book will provide a practical CPD programme, one that directly looks at bias and some of 'the roots of bias'. As mentioned earlier, **some staff and helpers might not realise that they are demonstrating unhelpful levels of bias, while others will know each and every time that they do it**[36] , they as well will often know their reasons and intentions for using bias in such unhelpful ways. **With 'bias' there are only 'those that benefit' and 'those that do not benefit'.**

Some Interesting Terms and Phrases to Consider and Discuss:

'Walking back'. A popular expression used to describe an individual and or groups desire to withdraw a potentially bad mistake or misstep (comment, policy, action, etc.) in the most efficient way possible and ideally with 'no blame' and or 'future victimising' going around. Some times within relationship challenges at work and or within the wider community, often it can be more 'efficient' to take this approach.

---

[36] This can be done 'overtly' (out in the 'open') or 'covertly' (behind closed doors).

Conclusion and Recommendations

Thank you so so very much for reading this book, we hope that you have enjoyed reading it as much as we have enjoyed writing it!

As mentioned in the beginning of this book, 'the knowing' more about yourself and the 'taking the ownership' of your lived experiences (and 'your reaction' to them) is part of self-help, self-awareness, self-care, and self-love.

Self-care hopefully is then on the same path and has the intention as does self-love, and self-discovery, and self-recovery.

Please take your time and do not rush to make any real in-depth changes. There is no 'timescale' or 'map', learning from any lived experience may take a relatively short period of time, or it may go onto to take a 'lifetime of disowning' and 'starting over' at times in order to just 'move forward'…only the universe knows (but she clearly wants to pass this self-awareness process on to you…to each of us, it is not meant to be kept 'a secret' that only some are able to access).

It has taken me decades to be able to clarify and re-clarify the existence of some of my own life experiences, then to 'learn and re-learn' from my own actions and non-actions and then to finally move towards 'making the best of my own now'.

I am sure that several of the readers could relate to this too…so take some time to exhale daily… our 'enlightened time', this coming to get to know ourselves, this will come, but taking more time to breathe will be a great and momentous start!

My mother told me years ago that sometimes the things that I feel and see each day could have nothing to do with us whatsoever, and that sometimes without 'instinctively knowing', we might actually be 'a vessel' for someone else's lived experiences and someone else's personal development.

The universe has its own way of giving us 'messages for life', this is very true for me too, where I thought (wrongly) that if I was open and humble 'enough', that together we (global beings) could effect change in most things, this was indeed a great intention but if global beings are really growing , really changing in their own times and in their own ways, then perhaps we could be wasting our time somewhat being judgemental , wasting time by 'watching the clock for change in others around us', we could be totally assessing certain global being 'moments and people' wrongly (and I really could have [for example] been focusing on me and my own reactions, my own non-actions and my own personal learning instead) without any blame, without any guilt and definitely without any shame.

In concluding this 'small' but hopefully a very 'pocket sized', worthwhile and practical opportunity we would like to leave you with a summary of some 'practical considerations take aways':

1. To know yourself, regardless of your age and your current circumstance is a valuable gift and a great future opportunity to assist you in making the best of 'the now' …it is your own life, take it.

2. Self-Help and Self-Development is like any opportunity; global beings will either use it or disuse it at their own pace and within their own frame of reference.

3. We can learn so much from our own mistakes.

4. A lived experience(s) can only grow into insights once triggered say by a memory or a 'collision of memories', a smell, taste, or an image in nature or in humanity, a day dream, etc. (and or reflections and or flashbacks of these moments).

   Usually these moments are not planned or scripted and they could be very unique to only us (although some Eurocentric therapy and analytic practices often take credit for unlocking these in individuals, couples, families, cultures, communities, countries, religions and the like).

5. *Even if no one else seems to care and or even if no one else seems to understand and or if no one else seems to value the lived experience(s) that you might personally carry and move with, **so what**…*it is very unreasonable to expect that they should 'automatically know you', you potentially have thrown some of these issues around in your heart and soul for quite a while now and they have not, and *if you can ever have ' a real moment' with another global being then please count yourself blessed.* Either way, do not see these people as your enemy or

as 'a non-friend'...*insight and intentions lead to further self-understanding.*

6. related to the above, do not be so quick to latch on to others 'labels' for you, especially those that may be about you and or to the definition(s) that others might 'attach' onto you and your lived experiences. Only deep and meaningful self-exploration will lead to real insights about any 'true definitions and naming of 'you' and your lived experiences'.

7. Do not be fooled by 'cultural appropriation experiences' either, sometimes people attached themselves to the parts of the cultures and the traditions of others for a variety of reasons, often directly rooted within them, and often related to their reactions to their own personal lived experience(s), self-esteem and or self-image.

8. Any 'over-connecting' to you/with you could easily be part of the cultural appropriation process, only time, meditation and reflections will lead to further clarity in your life...insightful caution can often be a wise and useful first step and can really help you to avoid needless misunderstandings in this area.

9. Global beings communications could be an opportunity for two-way dialogue and exploration (for example). If someone claims that they wish to help you, then please also consider being open, to give 'humble space', and give some non-rushed time to learn about them too, 'the other'.

10. Not all 'helpers' are open to 'share in-the-moment' for a variety of reasons, often with good intentions (such as filters and other protections such 'as

professional boundaries'). If after a reasonable period however and you are still unclear of the 'intentions of the other(s)', you may wish 'to set pause' and simply take stock of your own hopes, and intentions for that relationship. Self-awareness as opposed to blaming others and or the misrepresentation of others that you do not currently understand (their motives and intentions), the latter might lead you down a path that you may not find useful and could easily 'distract you from your own now' and cause many more problems that you might not easily 'back away' from.

11. Getting assistance from others can often be very practical, genuine, gracious, and heartfelt.

Getting assistance from others, as mentioned above can be very confusing at times when you are unsure of the 'other(s)' intentions. *Sometimes, although not always easy to admit (to ourselves especially) , we may be 'emotionally vulnerable' or 'emotionally not available' in-this-moment and or could possibly have moments where we temporarily lack emotional intelligence to make the best of opportunities on offer* (for example, being unsure of what it is like for others to be around us when we might be feeling happy, sad, distraught, loved, unloved, like we are in/recently out of 'a trauma', when we feel heard/unheard, when our efforts are received/ not taken up, part of/not part of, harassed, unfairly treated, proud, hopeful/not hopeful, calm, afraid, like a pretender, like a survivor/victim, trapped, funny, confident/confused, vulnerable, aggressive, etc.) *even when there could be a genuine and pure intentioned professional and or maybe even non-professional assistance 'around us' and or 'being offered to us on a voluntary and or non-voluntary basis'. 'Contradictions' are part of life's experiences for us all.*

12. **As 'a helper', maybe try considering some of this books themes , especially the sections that explore the need to consider and reconsider our own intentions…a supervisor and management team are and can be very much valuable helpers too.**

Supervisor, management, and good allies can help to keep their friend or supportee on a positive pathway by not 'leading them by our own personal hopes and expectations'…even with good intentions you could make situations 'cloudy' and very complicated.

Remember from the chapter on this book assumptions, that even 'a beautiful life' can have or have had terrible and or traumatic moments within it and vise versa, an individual's life that is 'self-perceived' as being terrible and or traumatic, they can potentially have 'beautiful moments' occur before, during and after too. Self-care, intentions and hope seem to play a factor in all cases.

Remember some of the very insightful comments from my poetry friends and associates e.g. "…what we experience during the day, what we dream about in the day and in the night…*our thoughts, our reactions and non-actions, these all belong to us* ('me' and 'I') even though at times *we might feel comfortable with projecting these on to 'others' rather than 'owning our own moments'..."*

13. There are literally billions on the planet that are experiencing 'their stuff' too, all lives matter, and global being compassion, unity and humility can work wonders and the lack of humility can often lead to 'inner and outer battles' that can be difficult at times to walk back.

14. This book author does not own these ideas and considerations; they have always existed in the objective and subjective realms of existence. I am only responsible to staking a claim to my existence, my ownership, and reactions to my life experiences. If others can benefit from my physical efforts, and or my verbal and written thoughts and discussions[37], then we both benefit, and then I am truly grateful for the opportunities.

Recommendations

- Take time each day that is just for you.
- Don't be afraid to question and or change your intentions.
- Taking time out 'to pause' an action, reaction and or even 'pause a relationship'(s) (in order to learn something) and this 'pause' need not be thought of as

---

[37] Including those from our very generous informal focus group members.

'the end of the world'…we can get through these moments.

- Meditate and or relax at least once per day (ideally with limited and or no distractions).
- Listen to your body when considering what types of food that you should eat, for leading to living and enjoying your best life.
- Limit caffeine and alcohol intake.
- Consider doing volunteer work.
- If currently doing volunteer work supervision consider and regularly reconsider 'what type of supervisor do you really want to be'.
- Do regular CPD activities that help to further develop you, that could lead to you being more employable and could lead to you knowing more about you and others.
- Celebrate getting to know and own some of your own lived experiences insights.
- Support others, if they allow you to. Your words, actions and inactions could be very a powerful and inspirational source. *Important to know when to back away* though and when to unconditionally give people back their 'lived experience space'.
- As mentioned throughout the book, if you are a 'helper', being on 'the outside' of any 'helping and caring relationship' , one that is not 'intimate' ,then this is not really 'the ideal place' to be when trying to experience this, 'the lived experiences of others'.

- This is useful advice for those that are championing others, those that are advocating for others and for those that are mentoring/coaching others, etc.

- Finally, a lot of global beings that receive support from **any organisation might need that same organisation to "...be clear and up front..." about any assumptions that they might have on us and or about us and or our lived experiences.** If we don't' they might use their own imaginations and create stories about you and or project onto you for themselves e.g. "...it must really be about my race... it must really be about my age...it must really be about my faith...it really must be about my size...it must really be about the fact that I am in a wheel chair...it really must be about my health...", etc..

Working With 'A Lived Experience'-
7 areas about 'A lived experience' that fellows should know about and or consider' (before starting and during their volunteer placements)

Example CPD Training Programme for Volunteer Fellows

Developed by: D E Lawrence (October 2021)

CPD Aims:

To provide mini 'composite' case studies for fellows to review and consider and make individual and group comment in the area of 'a lived experience'.

- It is hoped that by fully participating in this CPD activity, volunteers/fellows will **increase their own personal awareness about their own lived experiences and enhance their empathy about others around them.**
- Finally, this awareness event could be used to make better use of any volunteer placements in the areas of communication, especially when **considering and creating 'beneficiary and fellow centred' and solution focused problem-solving opportunities.**

CPD Format[38]:

- Pre-reading of the text *Owning, Growing and Being*: A lived experiences and challenges for living, loving and surviving in 'the now', by D E Lawrence. *Some readers say that this book can be read and understood in less than 3-4 hours. This even included 1-2 nice hot drink breaks.*
- Audio, electronic and or paper based 'trigger' paper
- Audio[39], electronic and or paper Based CPD activity
- Participant personal action plan

Minimum Joining Requirements: Intern and or volunteer in a placement

Introduction to the Trainer:

D E Lawrence has been a trainer, author, and advisor for several years within the US, UK, EU and the Caribbean. His current interests involve working with and through issues of human diversity, equality and inclusion, special education needs (sports, performing arts and employability), staff Team

---

[38] There is also a small booklet: **Owning, Growing and Being: A lived experience and challenges for living, loving, and surviving in 'the now',** *by D. E. Lawrence (December 2021). This book takes approximately 30-40 mins to read. It could be read before, during and or after completing this CPD programme.*

[39] audio CPD podcast duration lasts between 15 -18 minutes.

and management coaching and the development of content for CPD programmes, bespoke training and programme content.

Presenter: Duncan Lawrence

Concept developed by: Laura Bradford and Duncan Lawrence

Draft Audio script developed by: Duncan Lawrence

Some Pre-Thought Questions: About 'Me'

1. What are you hoping from today's CPD session?

1.1. Had you had training in this area before? Y/N Explain.

2. What makes you 'special or unique' to someone that knows you the best?

3. What are your top three 'lived experiences', say experiences that make you 'you'?

4. Do any of these 'lived experiences' help and our hinder us? Y/N explain

5. Does anyone else know about any of your answers listed in questions 1, 2, 3, and 4?

Y/N Explain.

---

1. An Introduction-Purpose of this Training Resource

(Podcast Audio SCRIPT ONLY)

My name is Duncan, when I am in trouble my mother calls me "…Duncan Eric…" but please, do call me "…Duncan…" today.

Today, please think of me in a way similar to maybe 'a bus driver'…safely taking you to your very diverse stops, but the bus always ends up in the same place, together …we all get to know a bit more about *'what thought we knew' about ourselves and* maybe we get to know a bit more about *others too*, say more than before we got onto 'the CPD bus'.

I have been driving 'the CPD Bus' safely for a long time, by supporting myself, individuals, families, teams, leaders, and their communities for several years in the areas of human diversity, equality, and inclusion…the US, the EU, and the Caribbean.

I think being a fellow is quite amazing and I applaud each and every one of you for either being one, and or for those that are thinking about becoming one and or for those that are already supporting 'Year Here' and its work…we welcome each and every one of us today!

Some Pre-Thought Questions: About 'Me'

Our fellows are multi-talented individuals with diverse experiences, with their own life moments and who are trying to support organisations that are primarily trying to address entrenched social problems, especially those problems with 'inequality roots'…wow, just talking about the work of 'Year Hear' reminds me of growing up as a child during the 60s when there was daily social upheaval related to 'race', the Vietnam war, poverty, inequality and the list could go on and on…a lot for any child to be exposed to…a lot for any family in any neighbourhood and a lot for any community projects then and for those that exist today.

What genuinely still amazes me to this day though is that a lot 'experiences' from 'one of those days' when maybe we and or our families and or even our full communities clearly struggled , there were days where we sometimes had very traumatic events and moments ,some that we may have even witnessed and or have been part of, in some of these same moments, moments in which we may have felt within our bodies, within our souls and spirits, maybe even for some of us as these experiences were experienced as headaches, maybe as sadness, maybe as anger, and sometimes even as confusion…a lot of us might have even been amazed when we might have 'fell down' at times (usually at what 'others' see and describe as perhaps 'the wrong time') *,but we usually and very often 'get back up…wow'* …to support our very decent friends and families…when we get back up to be 'the husbands, the fathers, the wives, the mothers, the carers, the partners, the friends, the inspiration to others, the shoulder to lean on…yes, even to become a fellow of 'year here'…yes, quite amazing and **I am so glad to be here with you all today**…some of the participants today , maybe with stories similar to mine, some perhaps with their 'own stories' that are totally different to my own…please be very very clear, **our lives and our experiences do matter regardless of whether they are from 'the past', in these 'current moments' and or within our ' possible futures'.**

Moving on, as fellows we need to be aware and or 're-remember that;

- Life can have so much diversity and richness, this at times, this **'diversity-in-life moments and humanity' will always cause 'a lived experiences' in us all** (even if some of these may not always affect us all of the time, say in negative and or positive ways), **some of these experiences are the type that will bring up a range of happy thoughts, some experiences that could even bring up thoughts that could be very traumatic and some could make us very angry and or sad, unhappy and even lead to confusing thoughts for us, for our families and maybe even within our communities.** Either way, these may not be our fault, but they clearly belong to us all.

  Our lived experiences make us who we are but do not have to define us…often understanding of this takes a while for us as global beings to own up to.

- Life can be hard… we all respond and adjust to it in our own ways. There is more than one way to grow and respond as a human being.

- Life can be satisfying
- Life can have hope
- Life can have joy
- Life can have opportunities to support others
- Life can have opportunities to be supported by others

Over the next few minutes, we will explore the topic of 'a Lived Experience' and consider **what that might look like and feel like for you and what it might feel like for those around you**, as a fellow and or as a very valuable partner organisation.

During our discussions please remember, **this session could be part of an 'induction and or a re-induction programme'** …its main aim includes maybe being a reminder to us all of what we are hoping to do this year within our volunteer efforts, helping us to think about what we might need for ourselves on a daily basis in order to continue to be the generous, focused fellows and or partner that we are, while also trying to live our own best lives, lives that have moments of hope and lives that have moments of joy.

Giving to others does not mean that we must forget about ourselves…Giving to others means that we might need 'a daily plan or strategy' just to get through the day (this is called 'self-care') and then still go home each day and still being ourselves…a person, a human being and good friend.

Please Note: Please feel free to pause this presentation to get a nice cup of tea or coffee or just to get a 'comfort break'.

2. Trying to define your lived experience[40]

I remember going into meetings recently either as an ally for someone or for a job- related meeting. One of the professionals in the room usually looks at me and acknowledged via a non-verbal language nod that I understood what they meant each time when they used the phrase 'lived experience' in a conversation about someone that I might have been an ally to and or when these same professional people were discussing something about me.

Initially I got very uncomfortable inside because I did not know what the #%!!! that they were talking about. They knew very little about the people that I was with and they knew even less about me. Why didn't they use the phrase 'lived experience' when they introduced themselves and or their role(s) to us???

My 'curiosity' continued to peak over the next few months about what I thought was 'a peculiar phrase'. In years past I would describe this as 'making limited assumptions based upon limited information' such as skin colour, language, body shape and or size, the way people might have been dressed, etc. but somehow I think these professionals might have meant something more than this.

There are other terms and phrases such as inter-sectionality e.g. Where race, class, gender, mental health and other individual characteristics 'intersect' with one another and overlap…another very interesting way of looking at the diversity and challenges for human beings in their daily lives.

---

[40] Adapted from… **'Owning, Growing and Being: A lived experience and challenges for living, loving, and surviving in 'the now', *by D. E. Lawrence (February 2022)'*.**

Following on, because I have love watching and listening to others especially when they think that no one is watching or listening…, some used the phrase 'a lived experience' when talking about themselves, while those around listening intently and with rarely challenging…it was like every participant in the discussion space (maybe over enjoying coffee/tea, etc.) knew that this phrase was somehow 'untouchable' and that it would be somehow disrespectful to somehow interject someone else's views, thoughts, and or insights into the discussion…very curious.

Having several poet friends, they were quite helpful here. Most often said that 'a lived experience' meant that you had developed 'your own road map' just from waking up each day and living, thinking, and experiencing…and these 'recollections and afterthoughts' were exclusively just yours…your lived experiences. For a lot of us we wake up to living, thinking, and experiencing things related to race, to sexuality, to gender, to class, health and physical concerns, to language challenges, to our learning styles and or difficulties, etc.

In this training, the term 'a lived experience' from my point of view [41] refers to 'accumulated experiences' from our daily life that may have brought on a deep and intense conscious and or unconscious physical and or emotional 'energy' such as related to trauma, stress, psychological fracturing, periods of elation, happiness, joy, anxiety, fear, confusion, physical distress, etc …I am sure that there are

---

[41] Adapted from… **'Owning, Growing and Being: A lived experience and challenges for living, loving, and surviving in 'the now', *by D. E. Lawrence (February 2022)'.***

other types of energies that I have missed…please let me know so I can update my notes.

In an 'ideal world', **the assumption is** (that for ourselves) **'I' have learned to acknowledge that certain experiences have actually happened within my own life** (some which could be 'positive' and or 'not so positively' experience[ed]) and that I can choose to use them for my own personal development or that I can choose to use them in my daily life if I so wish.

Often for some of us, these experiences can (and might) block, predict, and or limit 'my' potential chances of happiness in my current life ('the now').

These 'issues' and or my way of thinking about them (often related to the past/present social, physical, emotive and or other related health and life challenges) may 'get in the way of the now' (where my perceptions of hope, happiness, joy, peace, 'so so ness', etc. reside).

Take a moment…what do you think about what I have said so far, does it make any sense to you and your life? Does it feel familiar to you? After reading the book , do you think that bias played a part in your lived experiences?

I have two real people, *Meema* and *Steve* (these are not their real names), in their own words they have volunteered to talk about their lived experiences with us all today.

Meema: "…These 'do gooders 'at times could make me forget about 'my past life solutions', and any answers that I might have had and or might have seen my significant others around me have/use. We have 'traditions' of not standing still, even during natural disasters back home… we get back up, culture is crucial and very important (to me) …"

Bias…not sure if this happened to me every day, but people in my offices seem to treat me 'different' when I don't have my six children with me and when then my partner drops them off to me at work, the office goes 'quiet'. I am never invited to many of the office drinks anymore and other women seem to look down on me, as if having children somehow 'makes me less than'. I am a married woman that loves her husband and her children, can't see why I should be treated differently at times.

To me bias is a lot worse than racism because people are quite clumsy with me with regard to me and my children and I have no control what so ever how they treat me.

Steve: "…As a white guy, I often thought that only 'people of colour' have lived experiences of racism, discrimination and bias…it took me a while to accept that I too have lived and I too have my own experiences too, some that still bother me now…"

Knowing about and owning our own individual lived experiences can be very confusing at times.

I agree with Meema, bias is awful and so unfair, I am sure some work places do not offer flexible work hours in order to keep single parents out of the workplaces.

I was not really sure what the difference was between bias and discrimination…now I understand that they are similar and a pattern than is built into 'the system' and helps some and hurts others. I am sure that I have been on both sides of the fence, from being helped to have been treated unfairly. As a volunteer, I guess I had always assumed that the service user's lives were always much worse than mine, and now as part of my training I realise that I shouldn't have assumed that and had no evidence whatsoever to back up that statement.

I shouldn't build myself up as being better nor should I feel sorry for people just because I am a voluntary support…very judgemental, I guess.

Meema: "…I worked hard in an all-white education environments most of my life, either as a student and or as a worker; I think I know white people better than they know themselves although most around me would never admit such a thing…".

3. What are you hoping to do/learn (today)?

In some cases, once a fellow is clear on 'what they want' and 'what they do not want' out of a placement, it is then much easier to plan and measure **'what is working well for me here'** and helps to then to **consider/reconsider 'what is working less well for me here'** (and how might I get back on track?).

For example, *Steve* says, "… when I first did volunteer work I was 'not settled' in myself and had a lot going on…I was unemployed for a while and my partner, and I were going through some bad communication problems. During this time, I felt very sorry for myself too and at times I wanted my placement to be like a 'permanent job' that I could make my name at, maybe even get the service users 'on my side'. Once my partner and I began couple counselling however I soon realised that I needed to grow up, spend more time investing into things that are important to me…I needed to 'talk the talk and walk the walk'.

Being 'all over the place' in myself carried over into all my relationships, I am surprised not just one friend or colleague ever set me down and said something like "…*Steve*, you need to settle down and sort yourself out man, we are really worried about you…"

Once I started investing into 'myself' even my volunteer work experience was much better, I became more clear and more focused, aware that I needed to be there for the benefit of my service users first and foremost and that I needed to continually work on communicating with and enjoying my partner…and myself …a balance…".

Meema: I was the opposite to *Steve*, sadly I was the coming across as the 'angry black woman' at my placement, I made others on the team feel insecure and not valued by me. Sure, my manager had a few issues of their own regarding 'race'…but I had a lifetime of negative experiences of racism, prejudice, and problem within my own culture too. I have a very very big heart when it comes to helping others, my 'everyday issues' especially after Trump got elected 'clouded' others from seeing the 'real me' and temporarily blocked my real love of people of any culture from coming out…I really want to help others and be shoulder to shoulder with them…"

Hopefully, we all can agree that **being clear and focused about what our volunteer work opportunities actually are** and or could be **is not always easy to define** and that sometimes our 'past and present life experiences' might temporarily (or longer) get in the way of our message and or of our focus …" …I am here to help, if you are not sure how I can help, please just ask me. I am here for you and personally I feel very positive and hopeful about our future work together, thank you!"

4. What are your support systems?

Another important area to think about is "**…who supports me…**in life, in my relationships, in my placement…**are there other areas that I might need support in?**"

Meema did a list:

"…I have my partner, my favourite Auntie, Jon and Mary my friends since secondary school (we meet up each month to eat and try to go to each other's 'special things' like weddings, etc.) and my two dogs Fred and Wilma…oops I forgot that I have Rash, my life coach for the past year…she is an amazing person and has been a good kick up the back side for me…"

Steve's lists included his partner of seven years, members of his five a side football team, a guy from his local pub and his couple's counsellor Terry?

For the next two minutes, I will just stop talking and I invite you to use this time to quietly make a mental or physical list of;

- **Who supports me?** Should I add or take away any names from this list?

- **Who do I support?** Should I add or take away any names from my list?
- **Who are my support systems within my** fellowship **placement?**

> Should I add or take away any names from my list?

5. Considering fellow(s): What types of problems may occur within your placements?

Steven: "…

- What if I get anxious at times and have 'flash backs' related to my past experiences?
- What if I have a disagreement with my placement manager?
- What if my manager does not wish to share about their own Lived Experiences?

Sometimes it seems like 1 am supposed to be a 'role model' for all white males?"

Meema: "…this is an easy question to answer;

- ✓ Placements that seem like they are not ready for me
- ✓ Fellows and their placements have different expectations
- ✓ Some fellows may have mental or emotional challenges
- ✓ Some of us walk in with 'chips on our shoulders'

- ✓ Fellows can't financially make being a volunteer work
- ✓ Sometimes the service users are racist, or sexist…"

Hilary-Voluntary Placement Manager with 10 years' experience: "…Some of my volunteers assumed that I didn't like them because I was jealous of them, and some seemed to think they worked much harder than I did and because of this that I somehow did not really care. They were so very wrong about me.

What my volunteers did not understand was, these service users at times had patterns of chaotic lives and that to address this that they needed support to normalise and to be predictable for their children, for themselves. We help parents to understand their part in their abuse (being a 'victim' meant that they had no power to keep themselves and their children safe) and support them to predict and prevent problems in their own lives before they can actually happen…sometimes the enemy is within.

I can understand that new volunteers are often naive and very committed to changing the world in a day…that was me and I am her, only ten years in the future.

Being a manager that has full liability and one that enjoys her job too, I have learned to delegate to others and share power and responsibility, to be patient and above all remember that I have a life too.

I try not to interfere with my supervisors and have seen the problems that sometime occurs when I have intervened in the past, I get them upset with me and the volunteers can sometimes project onto me, ' that only I care…that only I can make a difference…yes things can get quite messy.

Having a monthly group practice coach and monthly 1-1 coaching seems to have worked a trick and we now seem to have a more pleasant and happier work environment.

It was foolish of me to think that I could understand everyone's lived experiences, especially if I am not actually supporting and sharing their new life insights and growth.

I have learned to let go more, have written a small book about my life, it was very hard at times but also very therapeutic…so glad that I did it.

Staff, volunteers and our women service users can read about me if they choose (not mandatory).

At times in our lives friends, family, other social and or psychological practitioners etc. only seem focus on 'our past' or 'present' lived issues 'social, emotive or health challenges' (for example) and often they rarely push me/you/others, rarely encourage me to get the most out of my current moments, while 'walking' with my past lived experiences…side by side or whichever way I/you/others could get the most out of 'my/our now' too.

6. Considering fellow(s): Some Creative and Respectful Solutions[42]

When trying to make good use of some of the information and ideas that we have discussed so far, **maybe we should 'pause'** and then to think of 'solutions to problems/difficulties' and 'creative ways' as an alternative to the placement potentially breaking down.

---

[42] Adapted from… **'Owning, Growing and Being: A lived experience and challenges for living, loving, and surviving in 'the now', *by D. E. Lawrence (February 2022)'*.**

- Daily living can be difficult and challenging at times but often the results of relationships with others (friends, families, colleagues, lovers, associates, careers, etc.) can be equally rewarding and can cause moments of joy and friendships.
- The best outcomes occur when there is atmosphere of 'mutual respect' and a genuine aim of a 'win-win' outcome.
- Never lose sight of the fact that even though we are genuinely here to 'be of service', we are ultimately here for the benefit of our service users.
- Often 'lateral thinking ideas' such as assertively allowing 'others' (that are not normally involved) to come up with 'win/win' solutions such having service users added to your organisations 'Fellowship Advisory Panel' and pick their brains from time to time. By not using fellows names where appropriate then creative and respectful answers may come up quite easily, while also developing the service user's confidence, trust ,and real-time usefulness to the organisation (as opposed to just being 'service users').
- Never instigate a 'hands off policy' to problem solving due to race, gender, sexuality, class, etc. We all are important and have 'lived experiences' with 'lived insights' that could be useful in any discussion and or any creative opportunities for solutions.

Steve: "...We tried this a few times, where black staff and black service users only problem solved for each other...it often made staff paranoid and resentful at times to be 'left out'. Where I can understand the genuine roots of this idea, often it limits discussions and the development of 'positive team work'…sometime 'together and sometime apart' seems to work better…like small 'action learning sets', ideas that had their roots in the 70/80s. We also had 'Safe Space' times, where there were no 'bosses' (we were all 'just people'), where any topic and solution ideas were heard and included in the discussions…"

- Related to the above, keep 'equal playing field' in any intense fights (where all have an equal status in creating solutions) without having to give up whatever makes us unique and defines our diversity, identity, and self-esteem. **Note**, this 'way of thinking' does not negate the organisations 'duty of care' responsibilities.

7. Considering fellow(s): Thinking about Sustainable Support Systems[43]

Sustainable means creating the groundwork for potential ideas, solutions and "…wow …that was a great idea! …" moments.

- Anti-Discriminatory Practice means that that we are all responsible for each other's safety…while 'we' can at times be the 'problem', we are always

---

[43] Adapted from… **'Owning, Growing and Being: A lived experience and challenges for living, loving, and surviving in 'the now', *by D. E. Lawrence (February 2022)'*.**

ultimately the 'resources' that could potentially benefit all within the organisation.

- The 'Safe Space' idea can grow and be sustained with each, and every brave act within it…try it out!

- Regular CPD activities and guest speakers and facilitators-'outside energy points' can help this area grow for individual fellows, the service users, their line managers and the wider partnership organisations.

Thanks for participating today and thanks to *Meema*, Hilary and *Steve's* …contributions!

---

1. What is your main takeaway from today's CPD Programme?
2. What did you think about the pre-reading Book?
3. How will you make use of your CPD in your workplace?